Something About Mary

by Michael Soper

for Mary Lou, Always

Other books by Michael Soper:

Xavier Wakes
Stepping Stones
Reversed
Decrypted
What Happens After You Flunk French?
Impressions
Confessions
100 Exceptional English-Language Poems
Tea, a Literary Sampler
Dead Poets, a Love Story
Valentines Twice a Year
Second Impressions

Mike Soper is a co-translator of
21st Century Chinese Poetry

Cover photo by Mary Lou Soper

Table of Contents

Into the Woods

Into the woods with my pruning shears
and an empty tub I go,
to where the limbs are tangled
and the thickest briars grow.

I snip and chop and fill the tub
while blood flies swarm and bite,
and when the tub is full of leaves,
I leave a shaft of light.

964 North Patrick Henry Drive

The homes in Dominion Hills were built shortly
after World War II. We moved into ours when I
was about a year old. I was born (I keep telling
the medics) 25 September 1946. That is nine
months after Christmas day, 1945. It is still the
biggest single birth date in US history. The war
was over, and the Baby Boom was on.

I believe I slept pretty well, but I was a
different sex from my sister, and my parents
wanted their own bedroom, so, they bought a
house. I believe it was under $20 thousand,
and the mortgage under 5%.

Eventually, these homes would sell for more than $400,000; they are inside the beltway, in Arlington County, near Washington, D.C.

If you want to see what "track housing" was, go have a look. Look closely. They are all identical, except the front doors alternate, left or right, every other house. Pairs of concrete driveway strips (just a little wider than a tire) were poured between the adjacent front and side doors. They are brick on the first floor, all the same brick, and shingle siding on the second floor. Those shingles were painted different colors. The roof shingles were probably all black, originally, but after some years, replacement shingles began to complement the siding colors. The builder did not provide landscaping, so shrubbery varied. Most people added window shutters. We added an awning above the front door, and a chain link fence. Gradually, the houses began to appear a bit different.

They all have full basements of poured concrete. The basement walls end about a foot above ground level, and so, there are concrete steps to the front and side doors. Three

5

windows across the top; my front window was above the front door. Two living room windows beside the front doors; my parents front windows were above those. We each had a side window, and my sister had a back window, so there was "cross ventilation". There was no air conditioning in those days. Every house had a brick fireplace and chimney.

The streets were paved, and there were sidewalks, street lights and storm sewers. Phone and electric wiring hung from telephone poles. Those poles, and the storm sewers, would be of considerable interest to the boys. There was natural gas, and every home had a gas furnace in the basement. Today, Mary Lou and I do not have sidewalks, street lights or storm sewers. Inside the front door was a coat closet, a small landing at the bottom of the stairs, and a side window. We eventually put a big box fan in that window, which is why I don't believe there was a side window at the top of the stairs, but there should have been. Just past the top of the stairs was the one and only bathroom – for four people. The floor was black linoleum with a matte finish and random delicate white streaks and swirls. If you squinted at that floor, you could make out little faces and creatures suggested by the black and white monster movies of the day. But with only one bathroom, there was not much time for floor gazing.

Across the hall from the bathroom, was the linen closet. My sister had several sleep-walking episodes as a little girl. In the scariest one, we found her standing in the opened front door. In the most comical, we found her sitting in the linen closet on a little step stool, holding a toilet plunger as though it were a royal scepter. Her eyes were open but she was sound asleep.

Continuing counter-clockwise around the hall: my sister's bedroom, my parent's, and my bedroom, with a play bench. The ceilings were only eight feet high, so, in order to climb the stairs, they had to notch the ceilings.
Those notches became play benches in every corresponding bedroom , with wall-board sides and floor-board tops. I built miniature brick buildings on my play bench until I was old enough for an aquarium.

Downstairs, proceeding clockwise, the living room, with its fireplace on the side wall, the dining room, with side and back windows, and a galley-sized kitchen. A few homes had side porches, in which case, the dining room side window became the door to the porch. The kitchens had a back window, a side window and a door leading to the basement stairs. Five steps down those stairs was a landing for the exterior side doors, next to the drive ways.

The basements had laundry tubs, where you could hook up a washing machine if you added a fuse to the fuse box and ran your own electric cable. No one had clothes dryers, everyone had clothes lines. All the basements had the same gas furnaces and water heaters, and three small windows surrounded by galvanized metal window wells.

As the children grew up, and needs expanded, all of the houses were modified in much the same ways. But while we are still small, let's explore the neighborhood. They did not name it Dominion Hills for nothing. Patrick Henry drive extends uphill all the way from Bon Air Park to Wilson Boulevard, except for one dip.

964 sits atop the first crest, before that little dip. For as much as our street climbed, it seems incredible that it was a valley with side streets rolling down into it. Our walk to school involved a steep climb up three blocks to the right before it finally leveled off. McKinley Elementary sits half way up or down a parallel long hill, McKinley Road.

My bedroom side window overlooked the park and up the next hill to Westover Baptist Church and Swanson Junior High. Around the corner from Swanson is Westover shopping center; beyond Wilson Boulevard and through some apartments is Wilson Shopping Center; and way down Wilson Boulevard, heading for town, is Clarendon, the administrative center of Arlington. I mention these places because we walked to all of them all the time, for a soda, to go bowling, to hang out with friends. But that came later; we started out inside the fence.

Quite a few homes had chain link fences around the back yards, those kept the youngest children safe, with minimal supervision. Only a few had fences, or hedges, around their front yards. My parents' excuse was that my sister was afraid of dogs, but really, my mother was afraid of dogs. And my father, for all his athleticism (and belligerence) was never confident around dogs. Big dogs lived outdoors in those days, and roamed and pooped, hence the fence.

The gate latches were at the top, so we could not operate them until we could reach them. After that, we were bound by parental stricture: Do not leave the yard ! Do not open the gate ! But then came first grade, and the gates to the world were opened. The fence explained most of the scuffs on my shoes. As a teenager, I could walk the top rail like a tight rope, and vault the fence without even touching it. The back fence supported a red rambling rose that extended almost to both corners, and bloomed copiously for two dozen years. Long after we were big, and leash laws had come into effect, it still did not occur to my parents to remove even the front section of the fence. When Mary Lou and I bought our first detached house, the first thing we did was take down a rickety old chain link fence. We were popular right away.

The dip that interrupted North Patrick Henry Drive's upward trudge was the perfect place to learn to ride a bike. My first bike had training wheels, but no brakes. The training wheels came off after a few days, but it was almost a year until I tried coasting down the big hills. The steepest was that three block climb to the right at the bottom of our dip. I knew that I could not jump the sidewalk curbs, so I walked my bike to the top of the hill, straddled it right in the middle of the street, and coasted down. It was like a roller coaster. I had no idea I could accelerate to 30 or 40 miles an hour. I could not stop the bike, but it coasted to a stop half way up the opposite hill, and I hopped off. I was delighted. But I tried my luck once too often: a car was coming down Patrick Henry Drive. I tilted to the left, and crossed in front of it, but crashed into the curb and broke my right arm. I did not know it was broken, neither did my mother, but my father took one look, and we headed for the hospital. While we were waiting for a doctor, an ambulance ran over a little boy in the parking lot. The child died "on the table", and there was lots of commotion in the hospital. They reset my broken bone. My arm hurt, and I was just learning to write, but I understood that I was the lucky boy that evening.

Our immediate neighbors were typical of the other homeowners. My father was a purchasing agent for the Government Printing Office. Frank, next door, was a minister of music. Frank, across the street, worked for the Bureau of Indian Affairs. Jake, next door, was a Navy Chief assigned to the Navy Department. Tom, behind us, was a public high school principal. Don, a few doors down, managed a grocery store for one of the big chains. There were several military officers, an FBI agent, an insurance salesman. Over the years, some of these men were trotted out as object lessons. The public schools downtown were getting so rough that gentle Tom feared for his life. The stress killed him before he could retire. *That's why we live in the suburbs, so you don't have to go to those schools.* As shop-lifting increased, Don's grocery store began to lose money. The chain closed it, and made no attempt to relocate Don, so he lost his pension. *That's what they do, abolish your job just before you can retire. That's why we work for the federal government. You need a college degree to work for the FBI. The military has some interesting jobs, but you have to move every three years.* Too true.

Rodney, my toy-soldiers buddy, moved away
when his Army officer dad was reassigned.
I never heard from him again.

I could not act, at the time, on all of this advice.
The draft, and a few bad grades, took me out of
college. Hiring freezes kept me out of the
government for some years. But I eventually
found work with the Department of Defense,
and so did Mary Lou. Her dad, my mother, my
brother-in-law, my uncles, all worked for the
government. Our oldest son is a fifth
generation federal employee. It's a company
town.

All of the younger brothers and sisters just
assumed that they would follow their siblings
into Swanson Junior High School. But then
they built Kenmore, and they needed to fill it
with pupils, and so we were bused away. We
were furious. "Let *them* go to Kenmore for
three years, and see how *they* like it!" Furious
but powerless, until our resentment found an
outlet – the buses. Around Halloween someone
discovered, probably by accident, that stubby
screwdrivers fit inside jacket pockets. And
right in front of him, and beside him, were all

these screws, just waiting, and he began to unscrew the bus. Within a few days, all of the buses from Dominion Hills were rolling rattle traps, with seat backs and side panels hanging by a couple of loosened screws.

If they had searched us, upon arrival, they would have caught us red handed. But the maintenance shop began filling all the empty holes with one-way security screws: you could tighten them, but you could not unscrew them. So, prison buses. Still, we understood that they had quietly done us a favor, and we stopped unscrewing around.

My mother re-entered the work force that year, so I had to get myself off to school. Sometimes, I missed the bus. But that bus ride was such a milk run, that if I ran through the park along the railroad tracks, and halfway across the county, and up a steep hill to Kenmore, I could some- times beat the bus. And that was the end of the baby fat. Three years later, we were back on track in Washington-Lee High School. My sister was a senior. We had some of our parents' teachers.

W&L also involved a school bus. Sometimes I got off in Westover and ate an entire pizza on the way home. When I got home, the newspapers were waiting for me. When I finished the first edition, about 60 houses, the second edition was waiting for me, another two dozen houses, all the way up to Wilson Boulevard. A pizza did not diminish my appetite for dinner one little bit.
I got to know every house in Dominion Hills, and all of their modifications.

When the original furnaces burned out, most people installed central air conditioning as part of the replacement. Anyone with children installed a bath and rec room in their basement, the plumbing was already roughed in. Once that basement storage space was gone, you had to use the attic, so you needed to replace the little hatch with pull-down stairs, and add some flooring, and an attic ventilation fan. As teenagers began to take showers, the original plastic tiles became unglued, so, use that new basement bathroom while the original upstairs bathroom finally gets some real tile. Not that a paper route gives you entry beyond the front door into your customers' homes, but you get to know the contractors' trucks, and anyway, you're talking to their kids. Little fuse boxes were replaced with bigger breaker boxes as clothes dryers and dishwashers were added. I imagine, after I left, that people replaced their old windows with insulated, double pane, vinyl windows – and kept them closed.

Central air conditioning changed the very character of Dominion Hills. The houses were so close together, and the windows were open seven months a year. When my father sneezed, the boys next door yelled Bless You. When David practiced his violin, it was better than when I practiced my trumpet. When Frank rehearsed, traffic literally stopped. If you argued, people heard it. One summer evening after dinner, Philip's mother called him in to clean up his room, Now! We saw his light go on. We saw his window screen open, and he started tossing toys out the window. These were toys he had outgrown, but we had not. What a thing ! It was raining toys.

Eventually, we replaced our old screen door with an aluminum and glass storm door. It had a shock absorber to protect the glass. But the old door was screen from top to bottom, with a great big spring, that could slam with a satisfying whang-whap sound. The awning – nobody else had an awning – kept the sun and rain out of the front door. We could open the front door and watch the evening thunder storms come rolling in, and smell the rain through the screen.

And you could sneak a cigarette in your bedroom, if you blew the smoke out the window screen. See what you're missing?

Two geniuses grew up in Dominion Hills, that I am aware of. David, the oldest of three boys next door, behaved and studied and became a physicist. Philip, the youngest of three boys across the street, became a Capitol Page, and then ran wild. By the time he should have been graduating from high school, he had knocked up his girlfriend and robbed a bank. It was his first felony, and he practically turned himself in making the rounds of local court houses to pay his traffic fines with the stolen cash. So he didn't get a very long sentence, and while he was in jail, he became an optician. When he got out, he found a job with Peoples Drug Stores, and he tried to reconcile with his bride.

She was living with his parents, in his old bedroom. But something went wrong. She wouldn't take him back. He stood in the front yard and shouted, Judy! Judy! and when she looked out the window, that same window that once rained toys, he blew his brains out.

We all played and went to school and grew up together. One boy became a cop, another boy a robber. One girl became a prostitute, her sister became a division chief. And all the houses, unperturbed, stood where they stood, and offered what shelter they could.

After 22 years, my parents finally moved. They bought my mother's sister's house on the other side of Westover. It was not much bigger or newer than the house they had. In fact, it was the smallest house in that neighborhood. But it was a nicer neighborhood of custom homes on wooded lots. This was where the bankers and doctors and lawyers lived. They offered 964, in turn, to my sister, and to me. But my sister was already settled in a small split level near a country club. And Mary Lou and I, ready to move out of our townhouse after four years and two boys, wanted something with an "open" floor plan and a bigger kitchen. They offered to hold the note, but I don't think I wanted that much help. So they simply sold it. They lived on Jefferson Street a few years, and then followed my mother's sisters to Leisure World. When the aunts and uncles began to fail, and my mother, ten years younger, could see a caregiver role emerging, they followed my father's printing and golfing buddies down to Orlando. My sister became the care giver; my mother never thanked her.

My parents lived in Orlando another 20-some years. When my father's health began to fail, they returned to northern Virginia to a condo in Green Springs, where my sister could look after them. My father died at age 93, a week shy of their 70th anniversary. They had bickered for 70 years. We think they were both determined to outlive the other so they could have their own way for a while. My mother is 96, and has moved into the nursing care unit. I visit her from North Carolina when I can. I don't think she remembers me, but I must seem familiar; she does not recoil if I give her a kiss. And, after all, I do look just like her. But it is

pointless to try to discuss finances or
medications.
I simply entertain her with some pillow talk.
I tell her that I have been up Patrick Henry
Drive, and 964 still has the green and white
striped awning, and she would not believe the
size of the oak and maple trees. I take her
through the old house, room by room,
describing everything, and she seems really
interested, but clearly, she does not remember.
Still, it's worth a try, you never know, so I ask
her, "Mom, at the top of the stairs, was there a
side window?"
She looks solemnly into my eyes and murmurs,
"I don't remember."

To China and Back

One of these months, I should go to China.
There's the rub; I still don't have a free month.
The distances are so vast, there is so much to
see, that a trip of less than a month would be
more tease than fulfillment. But, it seems that I
have done the next best thing. I sent a poem to
China, to a bilingual magazine. Here is the
poem:

Oriental Valentine

The blossom petals of the Chinese trees
describe the tints and textures of your skin.
Enchanted lakes, rippling in the breeze,
suggest how feelings quicken deep within.
But lunar calendars do not contain
a day to tell your Valentine your wish.
The dragon boats all race around in vain,
the poet does not surface on his fish.
Confucius wouldn't ever recommend
I celebrate a romance with my wife.
Still, Rabbit in the Moon will always blend
the ink that can bestow immortal life.
My own red paper couplets are unfurled.
They read about you halfway round the world.

Editor Leslie Ping, in the introduction to her
translation, wrote: This poem has been
specially written to mark Qi Xi Festival – the
Chinese version of St. Valentine's Day . . .
 I did? What is Qi Xi Festival? But first,
to translate her Chinese version back into
English. It reads:

Eastern Sweetheart Verse

Rich crimson branch tips tell
of your utmost delicate skin.
Repeated ripples write my fluttering affections.
Do moon calendars include such a day,
my heart's inner feelings to disclose?
Why do dragon boats compete?
The poet does not again emerge from the river.
Old Confucius is certainly not pleased
   to see me
celebrate a loving marriage with my
   honorable wife.
Moon Rabbit, nevertheless, does not
   stop stirring
the celebrated verse-inspiring ink.
My red scrolls, unrolled beside the door,
Sing of you, ma'am, thousands of miles away.

She did capture the spirit of the thing.
She transliterated Michael Soper into four
characters, Mai-chu So-p'o, which can be
translated: Journey through verses.
   Search the hillsides. I *like* it.
But what is Qi Xi Festival? On the seventh
night of the seventh month, the Oxherd and the
Weaver Maid are re-united.

There are several versions of the story,
which suggested another poem:

Oxherd & Weaver Maid

The seventh moon, the seventh eve,
the lovers' constellations cross.
They have one night of ecstasy,
and then another year of loss.

Were we given such a choice,
would we bonds and orbits sever,
and drift apart eternally,
to have one night each year forever?

Once, I sent a poem to China.
It came back with dividends.

Nalan Xingde -- Three Poems
Translations by Mike Soper

Far Away Thoughts
by Nalan Xingde

A steep march, a wet march,
going to Elm Tree Pass.

Along this path, through the night:
the sounds of a thousand tents.
More wind, more snow.
In broken dreams,
the sounds of the country
and the old garden
are not like these.

Manchurian, Nalan Xingde, 1655-1685, was the
son of Qing dynasty prime minister, Mingzhu.
He passed the civil service exam to become
personal guard to the Emperor. Skilled soldier
and poet, he was undone by the death of
his bride.

Soaking the Garden in Spring
by Nalan Xingde

Floating through life in a blink,
as unfortunate as this,
unable to forget.
Remembering leisure
on the embroidered bed,
and drifting blossoms,
resting on the curve
of a carved railing
leaning together into the sun.

Good dreams, difficult to leave,
poetry, powerless to reunite,
too much grief for one life.
Unable to examine
your whirl-away spirit,
I neglect my appearance.
Searching again the boundless sky,
morning brings frost on thin hair.
A mortal man implores Heaven:
Terminate my fate!
Spring flowers, Autumn moon,
reach an end, return to grief.
A contract for marriage
flutters, frightens, falls.
A pair of Mandarin Ducks,
steadfast, freeze.
Truly hopeless,
rain, reverberating on the eaves,
echoes my despair.

Nalan Xingde After 300 Years
by Zhou Nan周南
Poetry Monthly, Beijing, June 1996

The confidence of a few brief years,
Death changes to bloody tears.
Cold from beyond the Great Wall blows.

The moon or a lantern on a curtain glows.
Lyrics are water given to drink.
Love is madness in which to sink.
Pull one thread from the tapestry:
Heaven delights in Nalan Xingde.

A Vanishing Valentine

14 August 2016

When valentines come twice a year,
we've played with Mary and with Anna.
We reached a cousin nowhere near;
we drove along the Susquehanna.

And you were planning our next trip;
and I was seeking sanctuary.
You'd like an ocean-going ship;
I would prefer a monastery,

therein to illuminate
these verses which make you immortal;
therein, alas, to ruminate:
What's happened to the network portal?

I *wrote* a valentine, I know –
I've no idea how these things go.

Treadmill

Trompin' along on your walkin' machine :

(tromp, tromp, tromp)

The walls are painted a bluish green,

(tromp, tromp, tromp)

way to the left is the news on the screen,

(tromp, tromp, tromp)

shades to the right have an ivory sheen,

(tromp, tromp, tromp)

takin' it fast, takin' it slow

(tromp, tromp, tromp)

with no particular place to go.

How Now Indeed

How fare my sonnets now, pray thee tell me?
How seem they on thy ipad and iphone?
How fare they on Facebook? "Like me!
  Sell Me!"
Or do I rot in Stratford all alone?

You rot I fear, Old Bard. You're dead,
  trust me;
Your lines are all too wordy and too long.
"Blah blah blah blah blah." It isn't just me;
And lovers, now, they sing a different song.

Oh what do students know, nowdays, ever?
And what on earth do lovers nowdays sing?
"Oh oh oh oh oh." Hey nonny? Never.
Forget thy verse, thy song:
  The Play's the Thing !

How like a bloated corpse your ego's
  swollen.
Despite your warning curse, your skull's
  been stolen!

Something about Mary

When we retired to Hertford North Carolina,
I was happy to discover a bible college near my
doctor's office in Elizabeth City. I was still
writing a book of poems about Saint Francis
Xavier, and I could imagine myself giving
poetry readings to theology majors. A good
religious poem can enliven a sermon just as
well as a hymn, and I had encountered some
wonderful poems. I wanted to share them. So I
began to hunt those poems down, and collect
them for a book I would call "Poetry Readings
for a Christian College". I wrote to the school
and proposed a few poetry readings for the
coming year. They never replied, but I
continued to search for religious poems; after
all, I have outlasted other administrations.

Now you would think that the best place to find
religious poems would be in anthologies of
religious poetry. I tried that. I purchased them,
I read them, and I was disappointed. It depends
on what passes for "religious". Typically, these
anthologies contain a half dozen of Shakes-
peare's poems on mortality, a half dozen
Wordsworth poems on nature, and a half dozen

each Irish and Scottish dialect poems about kindly parsons, but they do not contain William Benet's *Whale,* Stephen Benet's *David,* Vachel Lindsay's *Esther,* William Blake's *England,* or Eunice Tietjens *Man Who Loved Mary.* Those I found in general anthologies or year books, all the more reason for compiling my own.

Several years went by. I published seven other books, and translated poems from Chinese to English for a dozen numbers of *21ˢᵗ Century Chinese Poetry.* I continued to find and annotate poems for my Christian anthology, but I began to have doubts: why was I abstracting from the internet? If someone really liked a poem, couldn't they look up the backstory themselves? Did I need to carry more coal to Newcastle? Then I discovered something: my books were listed on Chinese Amazon. I had no idea! *Xavier Wakes,* a book of Christian poems, for sale, in China! No one was buying them, but I could. I began to purchase and ship a half dozen books at a time to various foreign-language bookstores in China's major cities. Consider them "advance copies". If the store owner notices that the books sell right away, he might order more copies. I could even make distribution to English departments in Chinese universities.

It is estimated that 300 million Chinese read English. Well, perhaps. I have been translating Chinese poems for a lot of years, but I can't do it without dictionaries. I think it's more likely that 300 million Chinese have studied English at some time in their lives. What better reading texts could we provide than lyric poetry? It is more interesting than prose. The rhythms show which syllables to stress; the rhyme schemes aid pronunciation.

The Chinese have The Bible. They have it in traditional characters, in simplified characters, they even have it in English, but they do not have Christian traditions. When I was growing up, I could turn on the radio, and hear songs like *Count Your Blessings,* and *How Great Thou Art.* I could go to amazing movies: *The Robe, Ben Hur, The Ten Commandments.* The mission- aries in China were all deported by 1949. There is nothing in their culture to point them to The Bible.

It occurred to me that I should abandon my Poetry Readings for a Christian College, and compile an anthology of religious lyric poetry for the Chinese instead. Of course, I couldn't call it Religious Poetry; it would be censored; it would not make it to Amazon.cn. I decided to call it *One Hundred Exceptional English-language Poems.*

Most of the anthologies sort the poems by year of publication. There is a problem with that. For my selection, that would imply that Christianity died a hundred years ago. It did not. Lyric poetry died. And so, I do not give dates in the book. I sorted the poems from Old Testament through the birth and life and resurrection of Christ and beyond, into the faith. But I don't use those headings, let the censors figure it out, or, hopefully, not.

So, now I have a new book, one with a better purpose. In "six to eight weeks" I will know if "extended distribution" will carry it onto Amazon.cn. I have bagged my old notes and manuscripts, and stowed them in a closet. I should rest; but I am restless. Do I have any regrets? Well, yes. I wanted to write something about Mary.

When you write about poets, you can ask whether certain events may have affected their outlook on life, you can analyze whether this or that friend may have influenced their style. But when you write about Mary – fools rush in – you ask if she really was "Ever Virgin" or if Christ had those brothers and sisters the Bible mentions. You ask if Mary herself is the result of a virgin birth, as some Catholics claim. You ask if she ascended bodily into heaven from Ephesus or fell asleep near her empty tomb at Mount Zion, which one? You ask if Catholics actually worship Mary. Here are questions of real substance for theology majors, but what about English majors? How does the subject, the contemplation of Mary, affect poets? The same way she affects artists and musicians: she transports them to new levels.

First example, Joyce Kilmer. You met him in the third grade. *Trees.* "Poems are made by fools like me, but only God can make a tree." And ever after, we've had contests: who can write the funniest parody of *Trees*? It's a shame really, he wrote much better poems. But his best was about Mary.

A Blue Valentine

Monsignore,
Right Reverend Bishop Valentinus,
Sometime of Interamna, which is called Ferni,
Now of the delightful Court of Heaven,
I respectfully salute you, I genuflect
And I kiss your episcopal ring.

It is not, Monsignore,
The fragrant memory of your holy life,
Nor that of your shining and joyous martyrdom,
Which causes me now to address you.
But since this is your august festival,
Monsignore,
It seems appropriate to me to state
According to a venerable and agreeable custom,
That I love a beautiful lady.
Her eyes, Monsignore,
Are so blue that they put lovely little blue
   reflections
On every thing that she looks at,
Such as a wall. or the moon, or my heart.

It is like light coming through blue stained
   glass,
Yet not quite like it

For the blueness is not transparent,
Only translucent.
Her soul's light shines through,
But her soul cannot be seen.
It is something elusive, whimsical, tender,
wanton, infantile, wise and noble.
She wears, Monsignore, a blue garment,
Made in the manner of the Japanese.
It is very blue –
I think that her eyes have made it more blue,
Sweetly staining it
As the pressure of her body has graciously
given it form.
Loving her, Monsignore,
I love all her attributes;
But I believe
That even if I did not love her
I should love the blueness of her eyes,
And her blue garment, made in the manner of
    the Japanese.

   Monsignore,
I have never before troubled you with a request.

The saints whose ears I chiefly worry with
    my pleas
Are the most exquisite and maternal Brigid,

Gallant Saint Stephen, who puts fire
   in my blood,
And your brother bishop, my patron,
The generous and jovial Saint Nicholas of Bari.
But, of your courtesy, Monsignore,
Do me this favor:
When you this morning make your way
To the Ivory Throne that bursts into bloom
   with roses
because of her who sits upon it,
When you come to pay your devoir to Our
Lady,
I beg you, say to her:
"Madame, a poor poet, one of your singing
   servants yet on earth,
Has asked me to say that at this moment he is
   especially grateful to you
For wearing a blue gown."

There, you see: subtle, worldly, sophisticated,
and yet devout. Who knew?

Let me try to answer one of the questions:
Do Catholics worship Mary? Catholics are
reluctant to approach God, Jesus or the Holy
Spirit directly. That trinity is just too almighty.

So they ask their priest, their patron saint, or
Mary to intercede: "Pray for me". Miracles
have been attributed to Mary, yet somehow, she
seems more receptive, more understanding.
One little girl dances, by way of prayer.

The Dancer in the Shrine

I am a dancer. When I pray
I do not gather thoughts with clumsy thread
Into poor phrases. Birds all have a way
Of singing home the truth that they are birds,
And so my loving litany is said
Without the aid of words.

I am a dancer. Under me
The floor dreams lapis lazuli,
With inlaid gems of every hue –
Mother o' pearl I tread like dew,
While at the window of her frame
Our Lady, of the hallowed name,
Leans on the sill. Gray saints glare down,
Too long by godliness entranced,
With piety of painted frown,
Who never danced –
But Oh, our Lady's quaint, arrested look
Remembers when she danced with bird

and brook,
Of wind and flower and innocence a part,
Before the rose of Jesus kissed her heart
And men heaped heavy prayers upon her breast.

She watches me with gladness half confessed
Who dare to gesture homage with my feet,
Or twinkle lacy steps of joy
To entertain the Holy Boy;
Who, laughing, pirouette and pass,
Translated by the colored glass,
To meanings infinitely sweet.
And though it is not much, I know,
To fan the incense to and fro
With skirt as flighty as a wing,
It seems Our Lady understands
The method of my worshipping
The hymns I'm lifting in my hands –

I am a dancer –

Amanda Benjamin Hall

I *would* say that only Catholic poets write
poems about Mary, but I am a Methodist, and I
have written two poems about Mary.

Reconsider Indiana

Saint Mary-of-the-Woods Indiana, 1842, the Sisters
of Providence have built a barn and filled it with their
first harvest. Anti-Catholics burned it in the night.
Sister Saint Francis Xavier fears divine retribution.

Reconsider Indiana !
Ere these ashes even cool,
comes another autumn morning,
come the children to the school.
And our neighbors come to ponder
what some ignorance has done.
And our barn was only lumber,
they will build another one.

Reconsider Indiana !
Though the storms rise in your breast
as you see our harvest smolder,
it is nothing. I attest
that here, in Indiana,
the good priest who brought me thence
has begun an institution
of enlightened reverence.
And Our Lady, loved and honored,
from atop its golden dome,
will smile down on Indiana
where her children find a home.

The editor of Notre Dame's press had refused
my manuscript for *Xavier Wakes*. Somehow,
that triggered this poem. Perhaps I was burning
their barn in effigy.

On Opposite Islands

Sister Xavier Berkeley, Daughter of Charity,
came to China in 1890; Mother of the House of Mercy,
she died in 1944 on Chusan Island, at the age of 83.

Everything belongs to God,
even on the Isle of Hell,
these hundreds of pagodas
where the bonzes with their idols dwell.

And everything belongs to God
on Sinkomen, across the way,
where nuns have brought the children
to celebrate a Holy Day.

They disembark, and two by two,
they come singing up the hill
in smocks of white with sashes blue;
their voices clear to Heaven trill.

And every one belongs to God.
Pilgrims with their loads of grief
trudge on up the hills of Hell,

and pay the price of their belief.

The children that they gave away,
now rejoice on Sinkomen.
Their parents pray for mercy still,
then, sadly, they descend again.

But everyone belongs to God,
and the Mother of all Mercies will
someday reunite us all
on an even higher hill.

If these two poems don't seem particularly
inspired, you only need to compare them to my
other poems in this book.

Perhaps I'm a Catholic sympathizer. My
Grandmother Maguire was Catholic, and her
daughters. My first cousin, John, is a priest,
and I get to question him: If Joseph was not
biologically involved in the birth of Jesus, why
do both genealogies in the gospels go,
indirectly, through Joseph, instead of Mary, to
Jesus? John says that Joseph and Mary were
cousins, both descended through common
ancestors from the House of David, so the
prophesies were fulfilled. Perhaps they were,

41

but wouldn't Mary be the logical choice? Then you wouldn't need an explanation.

And what about this story, that Mary resulted from a virgin birth? That, he said, *is* just a story. In the apocryphal books *The First Gospel of James*, and *The Gospel of Nativity of Mary*, the writers copied the Old Testament story of Hannah and her conception of Samuel, changing Hannah to Anne and Samuel to Mary. This story became so popular that the church had to issue an edict, in 1677, to declare it an error. It doesn't help that the Catholic teaching that "Mary Immaculate" was "born without sin" (absolved of original sin in advance) seems to imply another virgin birth. Yes, it's complicated. And the story, officially discredited or not, results in the veneration of the mother of Mary, Saint Anne.

The Glove-Worker

I love to dream of good Saint Anne.
She knitted gloves all day,
And she was called the knitting saint,
I've heard the glovers say.
She was a very holy saint,

Holier than any other,
Because she was of double grace,
Being mother of His Mother.
She never knew of tempered steel,
Of power-press, and never
Of trank and die and overseam,
Of table-cut and lever.
But often, when I've worked as hard
As any human can,
I see her with a half-knit glove,
Moving her needles, and I love
To dream of good Saint Anne.

I dreamed so much of good Saint Anne
All Christmas night, I knew
It was herself, and not Christ's mother
Nearer and nearer drew.
She held her Grandchild in her arms,
And softly through the air

Shimmering flakes of snow came down
And sat upon His hair.

I tried to keep from going too near
Such holiness and brightness;
I tried to keep my calloused hands
From touching His star-whiteness.

Then good Saint Anne she turned to me !
More wonder – she was talking !
She said how far from home they were,
And would I hold the Child for her,
As she was tired from walking !

Agnes Lee

Brothers and sisters are mentioned in Matthew,
Mark, John, and The Acts. How can Mary be
"Ever Virgin"? First, there are extra-biblical
accounts that Joseph, an older man, was a
widower with children, thus *half* brothers and
sisters. Second, there is no word for cousin in
Hebrew or Aramaic, so the words for brother or
sister were used for cousins of Jesus.

Here is Rupert Brooke's account of
The Annunciation:

Mary and Gabriel

Young Mary, loitering once her garden way,
Felt a warm splendor grow in the April day,
As wine that blushes water through. And soon,
Out of the gold air of the afternoon,
One knelt before her: hair he had, or fire,
Bound back above his ears with golden wire,

Baring the eager marble of his face.
Not man's nor woman's was the grace
Rounding the limbs beneath that robe of white,
and lighting the eyes with changeless light,
Incurious. Calm as his wings, and fair,
That presence filled the garden.
She stood there, saying,
"What would you, Sir?" He told his word
"Blessed art thou of women!" Half she heard,
Hands folded and face bowed,
half long had known,
The message of that clear and holy tone,
That fluttered hot sweet sobs about her heart;
Such serene tidings moved such human smart.
Her breath came quick as little flakes of snow.
Her hands crept up her breast.
She did but know it was not hers.
She felt a trembling stir
Within her body, a will too strong for her
That held and filled and mastered all.
With eyes closed,
And a thousand soft short broken sighs,
She gave submission; fearful, meek, and glad.
She wished to speak. Under her breasts she had
Such multitudinous burnings, to and fro,
And throbs not understood; she did not know

If they were hurt or joy for her; but only
That she was grown strange to herself,
  half lonely,
All wonderful, filled full of pains to come
And thoughts she dare not think, swift thoughts
  and dumb,
Human, and quaint, her own, yet very far,
Divine, dear, terrible, familiar . . .
Her heart was faint for telling; to relate
Her limbs' sweet treachery, her strange high
  estate,
Over and over, whispering, half revealing,
Weeping; and so find kindness to her healing.
'Twixt tears and laughter, panic hurrying her,
She raised her eyes to that fair messenger.
He knelt unmoved, immortal; with his eyes
Gazing beyond her, calm to the calm skies;
Radiant, untroubled in his wisdom, kind.
His sheaf of lilies stirred not in the wind.
How should she, pitiful with mortality,
Try the wide peace of that felicity
With ripples of her perplexed shaken heart,
And hints of human ecstasy, human smart,
And whispers of the lonely weight she bore,
And how her womb within was hers no more
And at length hers? Being tired, she bowed

her head;
And said, "So be it!" The great wings spread
Showering glory on the fields, and fire.
The air, singing, bore him up, and higher,
Unswerving, unreluctant. Soon he shone
A gold speck in the gold skies; then was gone.
The air was colder, and grey. She stood alone.

It is remarkable that this reputed heartbreaker
wrote the most sensitive poem about Mary that
we have, every sigh, every flutter, and all from
her point of view.

Rearing Jesus could not have been easy.
In another poem, Mary finally spanks baby
Jesus for insisting "I am God", instead of
burbling goo goo. Robert Wolf describes Jesus
in public a few years older.

The Son

When Jesus was a child, did people say,
"Oh, yes, I talked that way when I was young"?
Did Joseph storm and Mary maybe pray
Repentance for his keen irreverent tongue?
And all the bearded elders of the land,
Did they not urge diplomacy and tact,

And tell Him one could make a *stronger* stand
By not mistaking pleasing dreams for *fact?*

They must have wagged imposing Jewish chins
In such disapprobation of that youth
That all His playmates shuddered at His sins,
While one gray crony – laying down the truth,
Predicted God would punish Him and send
The gallows, or the cross, or some bad end.

When he was eleven, Conrad Aiken heard
gunshots and discovered his father had killed
his mother, then himself. Understandably,
Conrad wrote some strange poems, but this
excerpt from Miracles, a verbal pieta, projects
serenity.

from *Miracles*

Twilight is spacious, near things in it seem far,
And distant things seem near.
Now in the green west hangs a yellow star.
And now across old waters you may hear
The profound gloom of bells among still trees,
Like a rolling of huge boulders beneath seas.

Silent as though in evening contemplation
Weaves the bat under the gathering stars.

Silent as dew we seek new incarnation,
Meditate new avatars.
In a clear dusk like this
Mary climbed up the hill to seek her son,
To lower him down from the cross, and kiss
The mauve wounds, every one.

Men with wings
In the dusk walked softly after her.
She did not see them, but may have felt
The winnowed air around her stir.
She did not see them, but may have known
Why her son's body was light as a little stone.
She may have guessed that other hands
   were there
Moving the watchful air.

Now, unless persuaded by searching music
Which suddenly opens the portals of the mind,
We guess no angels,
And are content to be blind.
Let us blow silver horns in the twilight.
And lift our hearts to the yellow star in the
green,
To find, perhaps, if while the dew is rising,
Clear things may not be seen.

Finally, I give you Eunice Tietjens. As an
editor of *Poetry Magazine,* she presided over
the transition from traditional, lyric poetry to
modern verse. But when she wrote a poem
about Mary, she wrote a long, touching, lyrical
poem, her personal best.

The Man Who Loved Mary

So living wearies you, as now it goes
In this far province? Friend, I understand.
Here in Jerusalem your alien nose
Itches for home.
You miss the somewhat over-grand
Marble and gilt pomposities of Rome,
Since these things are your life. But as for me,
Being a Jew, I love this ancient city
Of forlorn hopes, of poverty and pity,
This sad Jerusalem, a-sprawl and dun,
Like an old turtle dozing in the sun,
Or like a face seamed with old suffering –
Yes, like a face I know . . .

Listen, my friend, since hours are slow tonight,
Perhaps a story, starting long ago
When I was young, a story of grey things
That once were golden bright,

And of a face scarred like Jerusalem . . .

Know then that I was born in Galilee,
In Nazareth, a town not over-free
From Jewry's troubles and the fruits of them.
You will not know it.
There I passed a yeasty youth,
Troubled with passion and with thought,
With a sore search for truth
That came to naught,
And a great love that left no trace to show it.

For there I saw the face. But it was then
Free from all scar, a lovely timeless flower,
Knowing no dew but love, no shower
Fiercer than dusk's "amen";
Holding its perfect cup
Trustfully up,
Like Rachel she was then – and yet not like –
not warm, nor dusky, as our women are
Commonly; more like a star
Clearer and cooler . . .

I asked for her in marriage, but her sire
Refused. I was too poor, too young;
Later perhaps . . . She sighed . . . and
    wistful hung
A teardrop on her lash.

So I left home for this Jerusalem, to hire
Myself to Caesar, hoping. How I fared,
Prospered and grew, learning from you
   of Rome,
From Egypt and from Greece the clear effect
Of some detachment of the intellect –
And how I grew in wealth, all this you know.

But I lost Mary. On a certain morning
Sharp as a crystal, there came warning
That she was pregnant – and betrothed.
Joseph of Nazareth, a carpenter. And so . . .

Then my father's death
Severed my ties with Nazareth,
And the years tightened their hold.

Sarah, my wife, is a good woman,
Jewish and proud and kindly – human;
Mother of daughters; faded now.

Of Mary I heard little. I was told
How she seemed happy with her carpenter,
And how sons followed the first.

And then one day I saw her.
I had gone on business to her town
And, feeling thirst,

Stopped at the public well –
and there she stood.
A youth was leaning down
Raising the bucket, and her eyes were fixed
In doting admiration, somehow mixed,
I thought, with awe, upon his bended head.

I wondered if she would
Remember me, and spoke. She turned
    and smiled,
Thinking of other days. And so we said
In a hot dusty weather
A casual word together.

Her face had deepened from the girlish flower
Into a wide serenity and power.
She was still beautiful, still clear and cool,
Though now I thought her beauty like a star
Reflected in an autumn pool,
Less eerie and less far,
More touched with earth, warmer and
    more alive,
Though still without a scar.

The boy had raised the bucket, and she laid
Her hand upon his shoulder. So they made
A group of filial piety. Her son was tall,
With something of her beauty. But a glow

Burned like hot embers in his eyes:
A strange look – a look that sometimes lies
Smoldering in my people, when the gall
Eats in too deep. I thought it boded ill.

They told me in the town the lad was queer,
That prophecy attended him at birth,
With signs and portents, various and clear,
Ranking him with the mighty of the earth.
You know our country people, how their griefs
Still breed the tangle of these old beliefs.
He took the tales to heart, so much was plain.
I feared for Mary, seeing grist for pain.

And so it proved. Her son lived out a story
Not seldom heard here in Judea,
The tale of one who thought himself Messiah.
For Mary's sake, I went to hear him preach
When he had won a little transient glory
And crowds attended him.
The man had reach,
And the deep-smoldering fire
I saw in youth had mounted higher.

A pity it is, all fire grows dim.
He came to grief at last, and died
Like any common robber, crucified.
It's no surprise you never heard of him.

I tell the tale only that you may see
What scarred the face
that meant so much to me.

For I have seen her face once more.
Today she came to find me, seeking aid
For a sad family of the poor
Who gave their all, believing in her son.
Now Mary succors them. I was afraid
To let her see my joy, that she had done
The simple thing, and come to me . . .

Joseph, it seems, is dead,
Her other children fledged and flown. She said,
Wearing a quiet dignity,
"'Tis not for long we ask your charity –
My son will come again to set us free."

And, O my friend, her face, her face!
It bears all human sorrow, all our dreams
Gone down to dust, all suffering, all disgrace,
As this my city bears them. Yet it gleams
Still with that star-like beauty, and I see,
In Mary's face, hope for eternity.

And so the story stops. I thank you, friend.
You have been patient. Night gives place
  to morrow.

The tale I tell you has no end –
Even as Jerusalem, even as sorrow . . .

I would not place the entire burden of Defender
of the Faith on my cousin, John, so I did some
research and found that, without hesitation,
without dodging a single question, his answers
matched Catholic doctrine every time. Good
man, John. But somehow these answers are
always "apocryphal", and too complex, and a
bit of a stretch. By contrast, the Protestant's
questions and objections are simplistic: "I read
it in the Bible!" "That isn't in the Bible!"
We've had a couple of centuries now to
develop an appreciation of each other's beliefs
– without much progress. It's only going to get
worse. Archeologists are digging for the family
bones, searching for DNA. If they find some,
the controversies will be intense.

So now I have written something about Mary.
Any more regrets? Well, there is one – but I
refuse to write about it. If you want to find out
why Vachel Lindsay wrote his fantastic poem
about Esther, you are just going to have to
break down and invite me to come give a
poetry reading.

Moro Rock
on a Smokey Day
with a Rattle Snake
before the Power Outage

The vistas could have been vaster.
The snake could have been a disaster.
But if we had killed it,
and skinned it, and grilled it,
we could have had dinner much faster.

Grrtrude

A statue of a bunny
hides a downspout grate
because of the war on rainage,
an EPA mandate.
Grrtrude,
in her certitude
that it was a live feline,
retreated and barged,
circled and charged,
like a shark
on a fishing line.

At the Urologist

While I was waiting for the Doc,
among his restless, aging flock,
reading another magazine,
I thought of when I was a teen.

Waiting for another Doc
was a lovely girl in a pretty frock
reading another magazine.
Your skin rebels when you're seventeen.

Every month, we each signed in,
and I would catch a glimpse again,
until the magazine descended
and my lonely adolescence ended.

Good things come to those who wait
but hardly ever come this late,
and so, I give the Doc a shout
as my fluids and my clock run out.

The Human Interface

I killed Rosemary; I admit it.
Not intentionally. Not bodily.
In fact, no one was more surprised when Gloria
called to tell me Rosemary was dead.
"What ?! How ?! Why ?!"
"Don't yell at *me*. *You* killed her."
And as soon as she said it, I knew I had done it.

Rosemary had not come to work.
She had not called in, she was not scheduled for
leave. They called her at home; she did not
answer. She lived alone, so they called
security. And someone had gone to her condo
and found her, in the bathtub. No blood, no
booze, no pills, just dead. An older woman,
worried to death, and I was the embodiment of
all her stress.

She didn't have to die. I am pretty easy to get
along with. And though I must have seemed
Change personified, Mary Lou will tell you that
I am a stick in the mud, and I will tell you that I
am the mud. But if you were a typesetter, come
the onslaught of word processing, you either
changed or lost your job.

I served my apprenticeship, and then worked, at the Washington Star. I was the last union-trained compositor in the city. Even as I learned the Linotype, the Star was using photo composition for display advertising. There would be a 50-year interval of paste-up between hot metal typesetting and computer-to-plate (or ink jet of acceptable quality). I would have been happy to work those fifty years at the Star, but they did something else to ease my transition; they went bankrupt.

The former Evening Star, and later Washington Star, did not go broke the same way that other newspapers are going broke, which is to say losing readership to television and then to internet blogs. No, they lost a decades-long war with the Washington Post. I never could figure that out, even as a business case study. Their pitch was straightforward and obvious: give us a third of your advertising, and we will keep The Post honest. But advertising rates are only one kind of dishonesty. Ads pay the bills, not subscriptions. But consider the contest from the reader's point of view: The Post is yesterday's news that you get the next morning and take to work with you to read on company time. The Evening Star was today's news that you read after dinner, on your own time. Maybe people liked the Post's writers or their political slant. I just don't know. But we all knew the end was coming.

And so, I went to school part time for a degree in Business Administration, with a minor in Information Systems. If computers were going to take over my trade, then I would have to control the computers. And I started applying for a replacement job. I applied to the Defense Intelligence Agency, for one. My mother had worked there. That would not get me a job, but at least I knew that there was such an agency, and that they had a Publication Division. The Division Chief, Ed, said he was interested, but he was up against a hiring freeze. He said to watch the Federal columns, and come back when the freeze is over – which is what I did.

But in the interim, I did something rash. I sold my "life-time guaranteed job" for a $25,000 buyout offer. I figured that the $18,000 after taxes would just about get us through a full-time semester, only a few courses short of the degree. It was a good thing I took the money,

The Star did not last the semester. Ed was able to hire me at the next higher grade, based on the additional college courses. And, at that second interview, he introduced me to Rosemary and the girls. They did not seem particularly happy to make my acquaintance.

It generally takes about a year to hire on. There is a backlog waiting for a security clearance. But I was previously cleared during submarine service. So, in about a month, I reported for duty. I just assumed that I would resume work in my trade. "That's what I thought too," said Ed, "but they don't want you. So I started thinking, what good, after nine years experience, would more typesetting do you? My vacant billets are in the print shop. Why not learn the rest of the trade? We'll be moving in a few years. Finish school; it will qualify you for some purchasing credentials. Then you can help me plan the new facilities. What do you say?"

What could I say? I worked in the old print shop, B Building, Arlington Hall for the next several years. I enjoyed it. I wrote poems about it. I could insert some of them here, but

I'm afraid I'm already guilty of too much "re-packaging". You could read them in *Stepping Stones* from Amazon. Based on sales-to-date, you would be acquiring the world's rarest book.

Within a few years, Mary Lou returned to work – DIA, Arlington Hall, A Building, as a Systems Programmer. The boys were tall enough to get their own glasses of water, and pretty good about getting themselves off to school. They could walk with the other neighborhood kids, so they were not going to miss a bus. We commuted together, ate lunch together, worked early and got home within an hour of the kids. Our co-workers were appalled. "Isn't this *way* too much togetherness?" "Oh Hell no.
We talk about you all the way home."

After a few years, I was promoted out of the print shop and into a cubicle. I had a title, System Manager, but there was no system, and that was my job, to bring in a Pagination System. Paste-up had labor costs, but it was totally flexible. Pagination systems were costly. If you made a mistake, you resorted to paste-up, but if the pages were correct, with maps and photos already in place, you saved labor in graphics and in pre-press. DIA put me through a few courses in government contract administration, and turned me loose.

This was to be a competitive acquisition. I would be responsible for writing the system requirements, the Request for Proposals, and the score sheets for technical evaluation. So I tried to interview Rosemary for her requirements for typesetting. She gave me an appointment, we met briefly, but she said, "This is too complicated, and I'm too busy. Give me your questions, and I'll answer them in writing. Is any of this classified?" It was not, which meant she could work on my survey at home. She seems to have done that. She gave me complete and thorough answers in a couple of days, along with some questions of her own.

At the time, this was cutting edge technology, so I had to travel to look at prototypes in development. I don't travel well, I don't like risks and promises, but I pushed on. We issued the Request for Proposals. We knew in advance that the resulting system would be comprised of cheaper terminals for text input or editing, and pricey large-screen workstations for the graphic displays. There would be a central computer, and a phototypesetter imaging and processing film 18 inches wide. So, we could go ahead with planning the new composing room for the new building while "acquisition" took place. That normally takes a year, after you have already budgeted for your purchase, and that is because there are multiple legal and security reviews.

Meanwhile, I was helping Ed plan the layout for the new printing plant and bindery. There would be new equipment for those as well. It was obvious that composition and graphics would merge – they would be sharing the same system. I thought I might become the chief of that branch.

We got some good proposals, and the best was just slightly more expensive than the rest, so we could, with copious paperwork, cost justify the difference. While the new building was being completed, I began to schedule our people for training on the new system with the system

developer. I asked Rosemary when she would like to go. "I'm not going," she replied. "I'm not an operator; I'm the editor."
"Ok," I said, "What about System Administrator training? Setting up new users, making backups of the work, changing file permissions, that sort of thing?"
"Nope," she said, "I'll let you worry about all that."
"Well, if you're going to edit, won't you need to know how to print off proofs?"
"Nope," she said, "they'll hand them to me."
"Very well," I said. (I learned that in the Navy.)

"Oh, she's going to retire," said Mary Lou. "Why would she commute six times as far, and supervise twice as many people, and learn a lot of new stuff when she's got to be in her seventies?" I agreed. But Rosemary did *not* retire; she went home and took a bath. Gloria was designated interim section chief, and in a few more months, we finally moved to the new building.

I had been working there for several weeks, supervising installation of new equipment.

The system was all in place and hooked together. I had been testing it, and defining users. I had questions. The system integrator was in Huntsville, the phototypesetter, a Monotype, was from Boston. They talk really fast in Boston; very slowly in Alabama. Their accents are way different, but it's the speed that gets you. Boston rattles on so fast you can't take notes. Alabama says "and – let – me – tell – you – " until you find yourself almost screaming into the phone "Tell me, tell me, tell me!" with your transmission lying on the rug.

Gloria began coming over in the middle of the day. We opened up new supply channels and ordered boxes of fan-fold computer paper, reels of magnetic tape, rolls of film, cases of developer and fixer. "Where are we supposed to hang our coats?" she asked. Then she called Brenda and said "Bring the coat rack – and bring the coffee pot!"

> Comes balloons and potted plants,
> sandwich crumbs and picnic ants,
> pictures and the old hat rack,
> souvenirs and bric-a-brac,

67

a Random House with tabs for thumbing,
all of this and more is coming.

And so they came, on a winter morning, before
the sun was up, complaining of the cold and the
long walk in from some outer parking lot.
And each one had a big pocketbook, and a big
shopping bag. The bags were full of family
pictures, coffee mugs, radios, cigarettes to
smoke outside, and, worst of all, hand lotion.
They bickered for a while over who would sit
where, and then they passed the hand lotion
around and lathered up. So much for the brand
new keyboards. I reeled from the room, and
ran right into Ed.

"You look a little rattled," Ed said. "How's
it going?"
"Oh, ok, I guess. The system is working, the
workers are working. But Ed, *one hour*, and I
don't even *recognize* the place! And *hand
lotion!* All over the new keyboards!"
"Well, get a grip," he said, "a good, slippery,
greasy grip."
"Aye, aye," I said. (I learned that in the Navy.)

If you've ever done any manual drafting, with T-squares and triangles, India ink and caliper pens leaking and smearing all over the place, then you can understand that the graphics troops were very enthusiastic about the new system. It was really an extension of an automated drafting system – perfect lines and joins every time.

The typesetters were not so enthused.
"How do you get an accent mark out of this thing? For a million dollars, it ought to at least do accent marks!"
"Well, let me see" I said, and I grabbed a likely reference manual. After an hour or two, I had it, a command string of two dozen characters. I showed them. "My God! Look at all that! We can't spend two hours on every accent mark!"
"Of course not. So, we store it, under the F1 key as F1,1, two strokes. Now let's print out this command, nice and big. Ok. These digit are the size, these two are the font, this is your choice of accent mark, the rest of this positions the mark over the previous letter. Let's change the font to Futura and store that as F1,2.

Two strokes. How many key strokes did you need on the old system?"

"Two strokes."

"There, you see. Print off a bunch of these and pass them around. If you wanted to play a little, you could figure out some special effects. The old system would have always given you the proportional accent mark over the previous character. Play with this and you could have a bunch of different, big, free-floating accent marks – to suggest profanity, for example."

"Profanity," they muttered.

But they were a resourceful crew. They eventually taught the system all kinds of tricks.

One concern we had was whether the graphic artists and typesetters would get along. Famously, it turned out. I taught each of them, in turn, how to load a new roll of film into the canister in the Monotype. It sat in its own dark room. You had to load film, by feel, in dim red light with the doors locked, to keep the room dark. Jack and Jill made a show of pairing off to go load new film together. There were some cat calls. They locked the doors. They turned off the light. Ten minutes passed. Through the air ducts, Jack asked "Can you feel it?"

"Hey!" we said. "We need some output!"

"I'm putting out!" Jill sang.

And Jack said, "She's *Really* Putting Out!"

"Good grief, it's *Saturday Night Live*,"
said Gloria.

Not commendable, but you had to laugh.

Three people could not be responsible for this group; Ed had to choose: Gloria from composition, Dennis from graphics, or me, the system manager. He chose Dennis.

"Good choice," I said, "But I'm about finished here. So, what's next?"

"Are you familiar with bar codes?" he asked.

"Like at the grocery store?"

"That's them, sort of. There might be a government version. Bar code applications are getting lots of write ups in management magazines. DIA has set aside some money for a bar code project – and we need a tracking system."

"Yes?"

"Yes. We have at least four dozen jobs in progress all the time, with pieces of those jobs scattered all over the place: half the text still being typeset, half the text being proofread, pictures over here, maps over there, and sometimes you have to find all of it and expedite the job because of current events."

"Yes?"

"But that's not all – it could be an estimating system. We scan all the pieces through all the stations, and collect the hours, and total them – and next time we know how many hours it takes to print it."

"Well – I think we could build the data base in our computer – we won't get approval for another one. I'm just not sure how the scanners would interface. But I could write the "schema" and the data entry screens and report generators. I did that in school. And we'll need ways to query the data base for a particular job, or a particular work area."

"Ok, give me a written description along those lines, with some wiggle room, and I'll use it to claim the bar code money. Your next system."

It was not all that difficult: interfaces were available from the bar code sub- system to our computer; the equipment was durable, accurate, easy to use, and not all that expensive; and I enjoyed writing the code. Everything was installed, tested and working. I had talked about the system, informally, with everyone while looking for places to put terminals. The day before going "live", I called a meeting in the bindery to tell them, officially, what the system would do, and what *they* were obliged to do.

"Say you come to work in prepress. You turn on your monitor. It displays the people who work there; you touch your name. It displays the jobs that are in prepress; you touch a job. It displays work activities in prepress; you touch plate making. You make plates for a few hours, then you want to do something else. You have a choice; you press Stop, or Complete. If you press Complete, that means you've made the plates for every negative in that jacket; and you carry the jacket to the next inbox listed on the jacket. Let's say you get a new jacket in *your* inbox; you use the reader, you scan the bar code, the job displays on your monitor. That is all there is to it. The system lets us track all the pieces of that book through production, and then it totals all the hours. Next time, we will know how many hours it takes to print the new edition."

No one said anything. Clearly they were waiting for someone to say something. Someone did. "And then," he said, "our section chiefs total our smoke breaks and our bathroom breaks, and compare the hours of production to eight hours a day, and find ways to lower our Evals."

"That can *not* happen," I promised. "The system collects hours to jobs, not to people. Personal activities are not defined. They cannot total what isn't there. Your secrets are safe with me. It's like they say about Las Vegas: What happens in the bathroom, stays in the bathroom." Finally, some smiles.

I reported to the Division Chief, "It's done. What's next?"
"Have you been reading about Quality Assurance?" he asked.
"Oh Lord."
"Congratulations," Ed said. "The agency has created two new branches, first new support branches in years, one for the photo lab, and one for printing. You are hereby promoted to Chief of our Quality Assurance Branch."
"But they've already pinched every spare penny out of your operation."

"Actually, it's not about money. You'll see. Are you familiar with Material Safety Data Sheets?"

"Somewhat. They've been showing up in the boxes."

"Good. We are supposed to read them and post them. We're going to install an eye-wash station. We have to list every chemical we use, and describe how we dispose of them. Henceforth, we report where and when we recycle our printing plates. And, internally, we need to formalize some of our procedures: Charlie sticks his head in the closet, looks around, and says to himself, yep, we got enough. But some of the boxes are empty, because someone was saving stock numbers, and then, incredibly, we run out of ink."

"Yes, that has happened."

"And we need to pay more attention to renewing maintenance contracts, and paying our bills."

"Amen."

"And here are your people." He pulled a list from his pocket.

"These are good people," I said.

"Yes: two system managers, two graphics editors, our regs and manuals editor, our color control engineer, and our cartographer. Below the line are some people who will work with you, but not for you, in press and bindery."

"When do I start?"

And so we became, officially, a *responsible* industrial operation. We verified that we were, in fact, draining into the photo lab's chem drains. We created check lists for various inventories. We developed schedules for every dollar and document required for every contract renewal. And I, personally, to my shame, approved the proof of the color cover that read: "Sixtieth Anniversary of Pear Harbor" – in 42-point type.

"Nothing lasts forever" does not begin to describe the galloping obsolescence of the current age. Digital imagery replaced our photo lab in about a dozen years, while printing plant volumes fell in half. Our publication recipients did not want to read encyclopedias, they wanted to search the data base. Our analyst offices did not want to update manuscripts; their time would be better spent updating their database.

The only holdup, in both cases, was acceptable prints. Once the color computer printers and networked copiers achieved good-enough resolution and color fidelity, the dance was over. The photo lab was converted to rooms full of cubicles. The publishing division was reorganized under the Information Systems Directorate, and my boss retired, and his job was abolished. I should have seen it coming.

He made a recommendation, on his way out, and for once upper management listened. "Reassign Mike Soper to contracting. Put him in charge of an agency-wide copier program. Do a competitive acquisition for a fleet of several hundred machines, and the competitive pricing will save a fortune. You can have dedicated contractor repair people assigned to the building – same day repairs, and much cheaper toner prices."

Clearly, Ed had been thinking of doing just that. For me, it solved a personal problem: Mary Lou already worked in Information Systems, and there was a rule in the agency that married couples could not work in the same directorate.

I had good relations with contracting, not so good with the computer folk: we had the only big computer outside of their control.

It took a couple of years to work through this. I had to locate every copier in the agency, and find out how, and how much it was used and who used it. The copiers were on wheels, and the agency liked to re-organize.

I determined that a fleet of a half-dozen kinds of copiers would do: combinations of large or small, color or black and white, stand-alone or computer connected. But I didn't just ask for speeds, capacities, and features; I required the bidders to disclose the dimensions, weight, heat, noise, and electrical consumption. One proposed brand of copiers, from Scandinavia, would have been exceptionally capable, but hot enough to heat empty warehouses – no doubt a plus in Scandinavia. It was a successful program, and yet, I knew it would result in that much less work for the print shop.

Meanwhile, Congress asked DIA how many contractors it had. Months later we were still revising the answer. If you don't store that information, as such, you can't retrieve it. In theory, whoever was doing security clearances for the Department of Defense should have been able to answer that, but there were, no doubt, several contractors doing those clearances, and not sharing information. And of course contractors were not in our records as employees. So the agency had to poll every office, compile a list, go back and delete the duplicates and verify spellings – it took months. Congress had a field day. "How can you tell us what's going on halfway around the world if you can't tell us what's going on in your own offices? Every system you have is a separate smoke stack! From now on, the intel community is going to use Commercial Off-the-Shelf Software!"

That might work, for unclassified applications like finance or contracting or personnel. In my experience it did not. But it certainly was not going to work for classified information. DIA employed some very bright people, and those people, over time, had written a lot of software to accomplish or support military intelligence operations. How were they going to port all of that into "commercial-off-the-shelf" applications – and secure it? I was guilty of building two smoke stacks myself. Mary Lou, ironically, had spent 20 years *connecting* "smoke stacks" as a systems programmer. An analyst could log onto a single terminal and query multiple data bases without being aware of transiting different computers running different operating systems. Her office was eliminated. She was reassigned to a systems requirements office. She said she felt like Jiminy Cricket, the only one with any corporate memory of past workarounds and remote computer operations. She knew all those users would be left in the lurch. DIA had a reduction in force, and Mary Lou was happy to get a buyout offer and early retirement.

When the Department of Homeland Security was formed, DIA was subjected to reorganization by consultants. I was invited to attend a management survey. "Did you know," the twenty-something facilitator asked, "that DIA has nearly half as many different job descriptions as employees?"
She seemed to imply that that was a bad thing, that we had been, somehow, inventing jobs for each other. "Oh, I don't know," someone mused, "a quarterback, a center, two guards,

a full back, two tackles, two receivers . . .
sounds about right."

"What do you manage?" she asked me.

"Copiers, and other contracts as assigned.
One each copier manager."

"I thought you were all branch chiefs."

"I was. I had a cartographer, a typographer, a photographer, two system managers, an illustrator, an editor – six job descriptions for seven people – a team." She did not respond to that, but continued on around the table.

We got the impression that DIA would wind up with some kind of "matrix management". We would have multiple responsibilities, but no authority. And, in the ranks of middle management, we would rotate. Somehow, confronting new challenges would improve all of us as managers.

"Aren't we, really, all of us, Decision Makers?" I responded: "Yes, but soldiers do it in blood, and farmers do it in mud, and sailors do it in the deep blue sea. The farmer in the dell and our comptroller might as well be living on different planets."

"Our comptroller does live on a different planet," someone chuckled.

That was all for one session.

I was not invited to any others.

Because the copier program suggests printing, the contracting office, short on space, had been content to let me stay in my cubicle in publications. One day, about a half hour early, everyone got up to leave.

"Where are you going?"

"There's a meeting in the bindery. The Deputy Chief of Information Systems is going to explain why our guy is going to be rotated out, and a software guy is going to manage the printing plant." I tagged along.

The equipment was silent, and the employees were standing in a ring around an open space. The Deputy Chief entered, a nice looking young man, well spoken. He began by complementing our plant manager, who was not present.

He reiterated the consultant's pitch about how rotation, in the middle ranks, would improve the future leadership for the agency. He said the new manager was exceptionally capable, unfailingly kind, well liked. He paused. I couldn't stand it. "We have not heard one negative thing about your contender," I said, "except that he has no printing experience whatsoever. No doubt he will want to rotate, and go from the obscurity of producing invisible software to the obscurity of producing the agency's only visible products, our publications. But what does our guy get? The obscurity of some contrived management position producing nothing. I can't speak for him, but I would not want it."

Without pausing for air, I plunged on: "Who is actually going to rotate in this agency? The analysts won't; they need a lifetime of experience in other lands and languages. Among the support troops, you can't rotate into contracting or personnel or security because they all require special credentials. These are, admittedly, artificial barriers to entry, but barriers none the less. That leaves printing. In 500 years, printing has not had barriers to entry – not at the owner level. You can borrow money, buy a building and equipment and go into business – and go broke on your very first job. That's what happened to Guttenberg. It's a beautiful Bible, but he had no idea how long it would take to produce it, or what it would cost. He lost everything. Your man is going to get phone calls in the night, and what can he say? Let's assume he's a quick study, and reads some books about printing: every one of these machines has its own quirks, its own favorite repairman and operator. And the operators – talk about quirky!" A few people smiled, and I concluded: "I suggest that you reconsider."

"Aren't you Mike Soper?" he asked.
"Yes."
"I thought you worked for contracting . . ."
"I do. I grew up in printing."
"I see. Any other comments?"
There were none. "Any questions?"
There were none. He spun around and walked back out the door.
I heard someone say "At least someone said something."
But there was no appreciative or congratulatory buzz about my little outburst. All of them had seen me run my mouth before. But they had

never seen DIA back away from a reorganization.

I was glad the day was over. I listened to classical music driving home. I suppose it helped a little, but I was upset. Not so much about the confrontation. He was twice my rank but half my age. I only spoke the truth, and I could have been a lot more indignant. It was not about what was said – it was what was *not* said. This new guy would be presiding over the demise of the printing plant. I had seen word processing overtake the front end of the printing trade, now I was witnessing databases and desktop printers overtake the back end. And all of our good people had skills that were not portable.

It was never a good match anyway, printing and military intelligence. Intelligence is restricted, and perishable. Printing, "the permanence of ink on paper", wants History and Poetry and Literature.

I was still shaky when I got home, so I took Molly for a walk. Molly, since she blew a valve in her heart, got her own walks, separate from our other two maniacs. Molly strolled

along at a soothing pace, and she would stop
now and then to remember and reminisce.
I hoped she did not have regrets.

"Molly," I said, "I don't know why I'm still
doing this." Molly's ears perked up.
"I've been working since I was fourteen,
fifty years. I could retire. I could draw social
security. I could spend more time with *you*."

Her tail started to wag, probably because I had
emphasized the word "you". We climbed the
hill and, slowly, the stairs to the front door.
I let her in and hung up her leash. I expected
her to head for her water bowl, but she stood
there staring at me, as though she were waiting
for further explanation.

"I don't want to be there when they shut
everything down. I loved it, Molly.
I loved all of it." Her tail started wagging.
Molly understood the word "love",
and I went upstairs to take a bath.

Poems Commemorating Xue Tao

translated by Michael Soper

Tang dynasty poetess Xue Tao (old romanization Hsueh T'ao) lived 768-831 a.d., and wrote under the name Hung Tu. She served eleven governors of Shu (Sichuan) as hostess, secretary, laureate, courtesan. Then she was retired to a suburban retreat on the Silk River, outside the capital, Chengdu, to share poems, entertain guests, and make high-quality note paper. There she is buried. Visitors still come to view her grave, her river-side poetry pavilion, and her well. Its waters moistened the pulp, and enchanted the paper for poets. These memorials are selected, from *River Tower Visits Record*, by Peng Yunsun 彭芸荪, Sichuan People's Publishing Agency, 1980. Hung Tu's poems and biography were presented in English by Genevieve Wimsatt in *A Well of Fragrant Waters*, John W. Luce Co., 1945, a wonderful book, sadly, out of print.

Xue Tao's life and loves were legend. Her lyrics stand apart. In one of her last poems, to

87

an old lover, she explained:

    "Each song has its own purpose and design,
    But mine alone are gossamer romances,
    Sighing for flowers beneath a clouded moon,
    Singing of willows' early morning dances.
    Like white jade treasured in deep secrecy
    These crimson songs have found a long
      abidance,
    Now, grown too frail to guard them,
      I consign
    To you our lyrics for your youngsters'
      guidance."
      Sending Old Poems to Yuan Chen,
        Wimsatt's translation.

Sent to Xue Tao

by Bai Juyi 白居易 an amiable Taiyuan man, who
served successively as History Lampoon, Governor of
Hunan, Minister of Punishments, and Book Distribution
Officer.

The mountains meet the clouds and sleet.
Your eyebrows arch to chase your bangs.
Bewildered suitors wander roads that don't
    arrive.
And still the Spring winds separate old Wuling
    from Chi.   [bygone cities]

For Whom ?
A Scene at the River Pavilion
by Xie Wuliang 谢无量

The River Pavilion.
A summer rain, light as dust.
The wandering poet returns –
a hundred feelings anew.
Holding a book, he recites aloud.
He smiles to himself.
The loquat blossoms have fallen,
and there is no one.

Xue Tao's Grave
by Dong Xince 董新策

Three feet of neglected earth, a sunken mound,
literary genius buried a thousand years.
In Spring, as before, the river ripples like
   bamboo.
This is Peach Blossom's encircling opening
   move.

The Empty Tower
by a predecessor 前人

The poem-writing tower, abandoned on the hill,

hidden by its deep and winding path,
regards returning banana and bamboo
as though they were its old remembered friends.

Visiting Xue Tao's Well
by Zheng Jiaxiang 郑家相
(Jiaxiang's writing remains to celebrate a scholar of the
first degree.)

Bricks lining the cold spring dissolve to
   jade-colored sand.
Poetry writing paper, like tea leaves in an
empty
   cup, might exaggerate.
I don't know if the Spring moon penetrates
   the grave,
but here are three double peach blossoms.

Water Dragon Song
Mourning at Xue Tao's Tomb
by Hu Yan 胡延

A wild cuckoo calls from the past.
The East Wind rises,
your dream is interrupted.

Here, in the cool Spring mist,
through the empty gate,

down the silent path,
to this sweet solitary tomb,
how many days have come?

Layers of mist rearrange the flowers;
a young peach bloomed long ago.

Suppose enchanted papers, dyed as before,
let poets compare praises?
Heartbroken lines tell how many.

In the bamboo, a red pagoda,
how small! Lean on the red railing,
the empty Well of Fragrant Waters smiles,
as if to say nothing of today.

Pine boughs and crab traps and
empty bottles moan vague melodies.

A green lantern tries to glow,
a silvery spring murmurs regrets,
endlessly desolate.

Release the Kind old Governor,
the loquat has withered away
and echoes old sorrows.

The Kind Old Governor was her first and last. Tang Dynasty provincial governors were reassigned every few years to keep them from acquiring a power base. Xue Tao bedded eleven governors in succession, beginning with Wei Kao, who appointed the young poetess, Secretary. But she rejected a twelfth governor, Liu Pi. He was furious, and banished her to a distant, barren land. When Liu Pi rose in revolt against the Emperor, Xue Tao was vindicated. The Emperor returned Governor Wei to restore order. He retrieved Xue Tao, and ensured that she was comfortably and securely retired, out of political danger, but not removed from her friends and admirers.

Eulogy for Our Mother

There should be 94 roses here. I haven't
counted them, but that's how many years she
lived.
You could say there are 95 roses here.
Her older sisters were Violet and Daisy;
Mom was supposed to be Rose.
Her younger older brother, Charles, (he became
Uncle Tweedle, somehow) wanted to date a
young lady named Mildred. He lobbied pretty
hard for the name, and he prevailed. His
Mildred did not last; ours went the distance,
94 years old and married for 70 years.
If you want to know the secret of her longevity,
I will tell you, in a few minutes.

They say, if you want to understand someone,
consider their friends. Who did she *choose* to
associate with? Evelyn Steger, Lorraine
Maffet, Margaret Helm, her sisters, and her
mother, Lena. You could not find a kinder,
sweeter group of women. So how do you
explain her husband, our father, Earl? Right
feisty was Earl. Perhaps he was enough
excitement for one lifetime, and so, she chose
such gentle friends. With Earl, she gave as

good as she got. He insulted her cooking once too often and she never cooked another thing – not ever. He had to cook for her.

94 years is a long time, but I wondered, what was her *best* time? She had two surviving older brothers and sisters. She was spoiled. But her best time must have been after my sister, Joy, was born. I've seen this four times, as Mary Lou, and Joy, and Anita, and Tiffany, in turn, had babies. Each became, for a while, the absolute center of the universe.
It was during World War II. Dad was deployed, and Daisy's husband too. Violet's husband worked for the Navy in town. They lived nearby. Millie and Daisy and Lena shared an apartment, and, with Violet's help, they *all* raised Joy. It must have been a special time for Joy, too. Too bad she can't remember it.

I have had two special times with my mother. The first was after Joy started to school. Believe it or not, Joy is two years older. Dad was at work all day. Mom and I were home alone, and lunch went on forever. It was the heyday of radio soap operas, back to back to back. Mom kept up with them all, plenty of time to grill cheese sandwiches. I got a little spoiled myself, and a little chubby, and when my turn came, I didn't want to go to school. The second special time was these last few years after Dad died. He enjoyed a challenge. If you could get cheaper long-distance minutes with a 16-digit credit card number, well, bring it on. Mom could not even *read* the numbers, much less remember them. He had some very modest investments that would generate 18-page forms 1099 by the end of a tax year. And he did his own taxes. And the CPA said they were essentially correct. But it was all too complicated for Mom. The computer accounts, the cell phones, the credit cards, they all had to go. Simplifying her finances was easy enough, as long as she could sign her name. She had a beautiful signature. But it did involve another round of long, leisurely lunches, just the two of us, trying to remember things.

If you endured some of the hour-long walks, with her walker, from her room to a waiting car, and the difficult acrobatics of getting her safely seated in the car, you would be amazed that once upon a time, she could dance fast dances, and she actually drove cars. When I

was the twins' age, she drove a heavy 1949
Chevy, with stick shift, and manual steering
and brakes. The trick, for her, at four foot ten,
was to see over the dash board and still reach
the foot pedals. She slid on and off a cushion,
but really she pretty much drove standing up –
but she drove – and danced.

Ask any of us who waited for Millie to get
dressed, or to finish eating. She was slow,
so slow that it was hard to remember: she was
a speed demon typist, and accurate. She could
spell very well. She learned shorthand, and
used it into her nineties. She was the queen of
abbreviations. It's a good thing that she did not
learn how to "text" on a cell phone: she could
have kept us all hoppin' with just her thumbs.

But I *was* surprised when she said she used to
play the piano. Rachel had begun to take
lessons. Mom said she had taken lessons too,
along with a girlfriend. She learned to read
music. She even played hymns for the church.
"I am astonished", I said, "I've never seen you
play the piano".
She explained that she stopped after her mother
died. Her mother had been so proud of her, that

it made her too sad to play anymore.
Eventually, she said, she even stopped going to
church, because she would hear those old
hymns, and it would make her miserable.

The saddest hymn, apparently, was The Old
Rugged Cross, because it was her mother's
favorite. Let's *not* try to sing it. But I would
like to read the last verse. As an aspiring poet
(66 years old and still aspiring), I can tell you
that even though we don't *buy* books of poetry,
we do not graduate, or marry, or bury our dead
without a poem. So, the verse:

To the old rugged cross, I will ever be true,
its shame and reproach gladly bear;
then He'll call me some day
to my home far away,
where His glory forever I'll share.
So I'll cherish the old rugged cross,
Till my trophies at last I lay down;
I will cling to the old rugged cross,
and exchange it some day for a crown.

That sounds like a plan. But it was a
mistake, I think, not to go to church.
The good Lord has already forgiven her.
Blessed are they that mourn, He said.

But, in not going to church, you miss out on the
second half of that Beatitude. Blessed are they
that mourn, for they shall be comforted.
The "Words of Comfort" were printed
in the back of her hymnal:
"Jesus said, I am the resurrection, and the life:
he that believeth in Me, though he were dead,
yet shall he live : and whosoever liveth and
believeth in Me shall never die."

And they are printed in the first hymn of my
hymnal:

> He speaks, and listening to his voice,
> New life the dead receive;
> The mournful, broken hearts rejoice;
> The humble poor, believe.   Amen.

We need to hear that. And now you want to
hear the secret of her longevity.
I will tell you. First, Bed Rest. Millie did not
believe in rigorous physical therapy,
in strenuous rehabilitation. She believed in
rest and recuperation. It's an old prescription.
It doesn't work for every condition or malady,
but, when you're not feeling well, it has its
charms. Second, great grand-daughters. Have
a little flock of them. They add years of

enjoyment to your life. And finally, diabetes notwithstanding: Do *not* skip dessert ! Amen.

Mom wanted to be buried with her mother and father, in Oakwood Cemetery, in Charlottes- ville, Virginia. Her cemetery records, which she had from Aunt Violet, date back to 1931, to the death of their father; they are over 80 years old. The corresponding city records were, them- selves, almost buried. They were handed down from the court house to the mayor's office to the department of parks. But she was correct: there is still an empty space in the family plot.

She will be buried there tomorrow afternoon. Charlottesville is a bit of a trek, but it's a trip that we have made together, many times before.

Tilt-a-Whirl

Where we stand, the earth
is spinning at 850 miles per hour.
Can you feel it ?
Meanwhile, it circles the sun
at 66,500 miles per hour,
while the sun circles the galactic center
at 514,000 miles per hour –
and these motions are additive.
No wonder I always feel a little dizzy,
and light-headed, perhaps because
the sun and moon aligned, combined,
lift the ocean thirty-two feet.
Three, two, one – liftoff.

Made in the USA
Middletown, DE
20 June 2023

32873677R00061